GRAY WHALES

THE WHALE DISCOVERY LIBRARY

Sarah Palmer

Illustrated by Sally Hadler

Rourke Enterprises, Inc.
Vero Beach, Florida 32964

Library of Congress Cataloging-in-Publication Data

Palmer, Sarah, 1955-
  Gray Whales.

  (The Whale discovery library)
  Includes index.
  Summary: Describes gray whales, where they live,
what they eat and their family life.
    1. Pacific gray whale—Juvenile literature.
[1. Pacific gray whale.   2. Whales]   I. Title.
II. Series: Palmer, Sarah, 1955-
Whale discovery library.
QL737.C425P34   1989   599.5'1   88-3242
ISBN 0-86592-477-5

TABLE OF CONTENTS

GRAY WHALES

Gray whales are very ugly. Their skin is covered in warts and pimples and is crusted with **barnacles**. You may have seen barnacles on the bottom of boats. Like humpback whales, gray whales suffer from **parasites** such as whale-lice. The whale-lice attach themselves to the whales' skin and feed on their blood.

Skin parasites make gray whales look ugly

HOW THEY LOOK

Gray whales may look strange, but their movements are very graceful. They are beautiful to watch as they swim. They twist and turn under the water with great ease. The medium-sized gray whales are about 45 feet long. They weigh around 20 tons. The female gray whales are larger than the males. Gray whales have no **dorsal fin** on their backs.

Gray whales are very graceful

WHERE THEY LIVE

Gray whales live in the North Pacific Ocean during the summer months. They like the freezing waters in the far north. Many gray whales live in the Beaufort Sea, north of Canada and Alaska. During the winter, some gray whales **migrate** down the west coast of the United States to California. Others travel towards Japan to the Sea of Okhotsk.

Gray whales like the freezing waters of the far north

WHAT THEY EAT

Like all **baleen** whales, gray whales eat small shrimp-like creatures called **krill**, and tiny plants known as **plankton**. The northern seas where they live are very rich with this food. The whales spend the summers eating huge amounts of krill and plankton. This builds up their thick layer of fat, or **blubber**, which keeps the whales warm. In winter the whales do not eat very much at all.

Gray whales use their baleen plates when feeding

Gray whales can grow to about 45 feet long

Gray whales have a thick layer of blubber

LIVING IN THE OCEAN

The gray whales' main enemies in the oceans are the cruel killer whales. These two whales follow the same migration route along the coast of California. The killer whales normally feed on salmon and other large fish. Sometimes they attack the gray whales. Killer whales are smaller than gray whales, but their huge teeth give them the advantage.

*Killer whales sometimes attack
gray whales*

BABY GRAY WHALES

Baby gray whales are born in the winter. At that time the gray whales are living in the oceans off California. The mother swims to shallow water close to land. There the **calf** is born in the warm and sheltered water. At birth the calf weighs well over a ton. It is 16 feet long. Many people travel to California to see the gray whales with their babies.

Baby gray whales are born in warm lagoons

GRAY WHALES AND PEOPLE

Female gray whales keep a very close watch on their calves. If people come too close, the mother gray whale takes action. She rams the boat to warn humans to stay away from her calf. But not even mother gray whales stopped the **whalers**. They killed hundreds of gray whales in the Californian **lagoons**.

Many people come to watch the gray whales and their calves

SAVING GRAY WHALES

The whalers found gray whales very easy to catch. They waited for them to come to the coast of California. There they could round up the mother and baby gray whales very quickly. At one time, people thought that there were no gray whaies left. Then some were seen in California, and the whalers were forbidden to kill them. Now there are more than 6,000 gray whales in our oceans.

Whalers found gray whales very easy to catch in the lagoons

FACT FILE

Common Name:	Gray Whale
Scientific Name:	Eschrichtius robustus
Type:	Baleen whale
Color:	Gray
Size:	average 45 feet
Weight:	up to 20 tons
Number in World:	18,000

Glossary

baleen whales (BAL een WHALES) — whales which have baleen plates instead of teeth

barnacles (BAR nac les) — small animals with hard shells that attach themselves to rocks, boats or whales

blubber (BLUB ber) — a thick layer of fat under a whale's skin

calf (CALF) — a young whale

dorsal fin (DOR sal FIN) — a fin on a whale's back

krill (KRILL) — tiny shrimp-like creatures on which whales feed

lagoons (la GOONS) — shallow bays

to migrate (MI grate) — to move from one place to another, usually at the same time each year

parasites (PAR a sites) — animals that depend on others for food without giving anything in return

plankton (PLANK ton) — tiny plants on which whales feed

whalers (WHAL ers) — people who hunt whales

INDEX